Animal World

THE LADYBUG

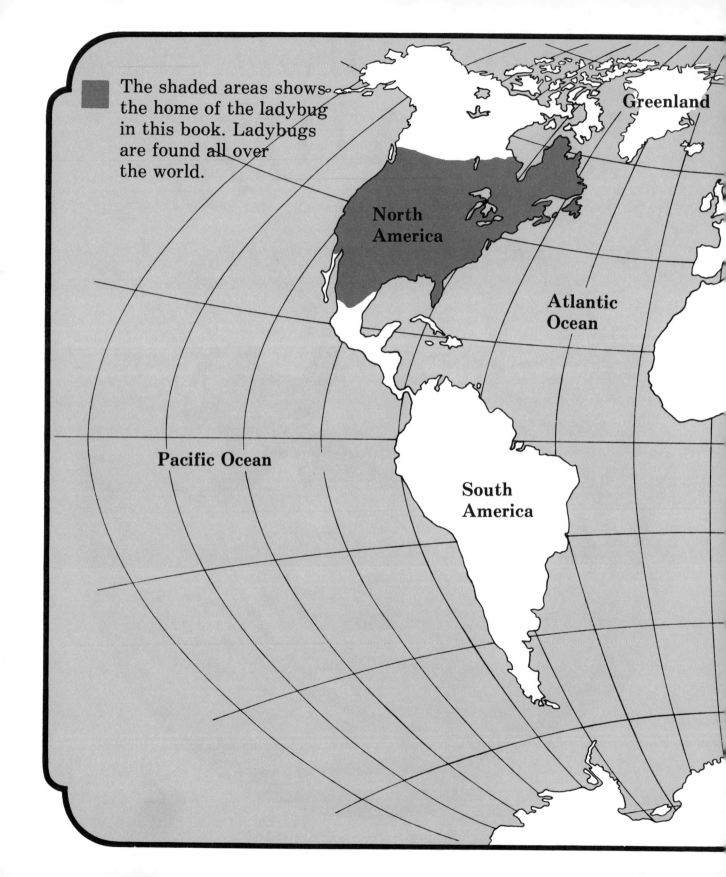

The shaded areas shows the home of the ladybug in this book. Ladybugs are found all over the world.

Greenland

North America

Atlantic Ocean

Pacific Ocean

South America

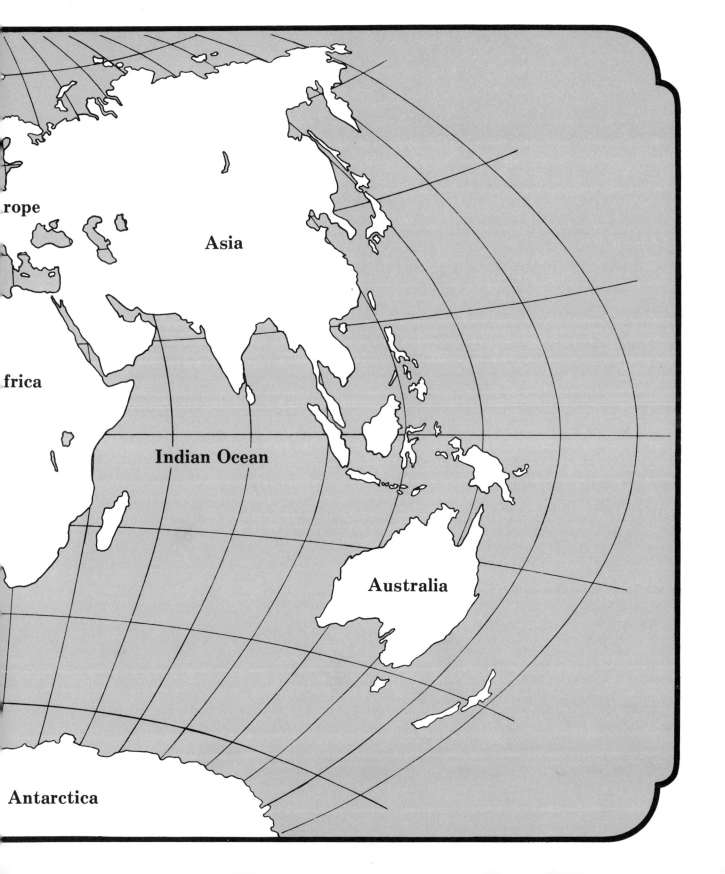

Year 2000 home library edition

Published by The Rourke Enterprises, Inc., P.O. Box 3328, Vero Beach, Florida 32964.

Library of Congress Cataloging in Publication Data

Pouyanne, Thérèse.
　The ladybug.

　(Animal world)
　Translation of: La coccinelle.
　Reprint. Originally published: The ladybird. London :
Macdonald Educational, 1978.
　Summary: Describes the natural environment, physical
characteristics, and behavior of the ladybird or ladybug,
an insect that helps protect crops by eating the harmful
greenfly.
　1. Ladybirds — Juvenile literature.　[1. Ladybugs.
2. Insects]　I. Shimada, Masako, ill.　II. Title.
III. Series.
QL596.C65P6813　1984　　　　　595.76'9　　　　　83-9750
ISBN 0-86592-863-0

Animal World
THE LADYBUG

illustrated by
Masako Shimada

This edition produced
exclusively for
A+ Child Development, Ltd.

ROURKE ENTERPRISES, INC.
Vero Beach, FL 32964

Garden discovery

It is easy to find one of these small insects in the garden. It crawls along the leaves of rosebushes or on bean plants. It is about the size of a small pea. It is nearly round in shape, hard as a pebble and colored bright red with seven black spots on its back.

The branch is covered with greenfly, and the ladybug stops now and then to wave its tiny antennae and eat one. When it reaches the end of the branch it stops for a moment. It raises the hard covering on its back, unfolds two small see-through wings and flies away.

This bright little insect is a ladybug. It begins life as an egg, so small that you can hardly see it. The eggs cannot be hatched unless they are kept warm. The ladybug does not sit on her eggs as a bird does. Instead, she lays them on the branch or leaf of a rosebush which will get plenty of sunlight.

She lays hundreds of eggs in several batches. Many will be eaten by birds, enough will survive. When the young come out of the eggs she does not feed them herself. She has taken care to put them near their favorite food. These are the greenfly that live on rose bushes.

The larva

The creature that comes out of the egg is unlike its mother. In the larva stage the ladybug is a very small, dull gray caterpillar with six legs and orange colored spots. Almost at once, it is able to wriggle and walk.

Let us look at it more closely. Its legs are short and are in the front part of its long body. It has strong jaws.

It finds all the food it needs in the vast numbers of greenfly on the leaf. The greenfly cannot defend themselves, so the larva takes them in its jaws and squeezes them dry. It may eat 20 or 30 in one day. It grows so fast that its skin becomes too small and has to be changed for a new one.

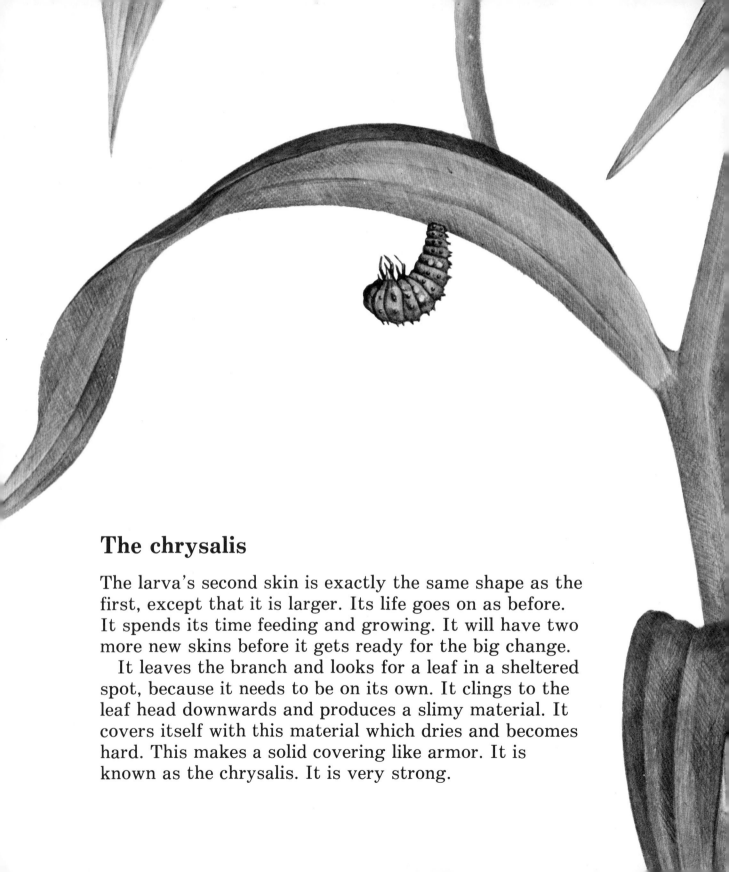

The chrysalis

The larva's second skin is exactly the same shape as the first, except that it is larger. Its life goes on as before. It spends its time feeding and growing. It will have two more new skins before it gets ready for the big change.

It leaves the branch and looks for a leaf in a sheltered spot, because it needs to be on its own. It clings to the leaf head downwards and produces a slimy material. It covers itself with this material which dries and becomes hard. This makes a solid covering like armor. It is known as the chrysalis. It is very strong.

Inside the chrysalis the ladybug larva has turned into a
ladybug pupa. It no longer moves or eats. It seems dead
but it is not. It is only asleep. It is being changed into a
new creature very different from a caterpillar.

If we could see through the hard shell we would be
surprised by what is happening. The big plump body is
dwindling away. The head is getting bigger and harder.
Two pairs of wings are being formed and the legs are
getting longer. Two short antennae are beginning to
appear.

These changes take about eight days. To a ladybug,
eight days are as long as a whole year to us.

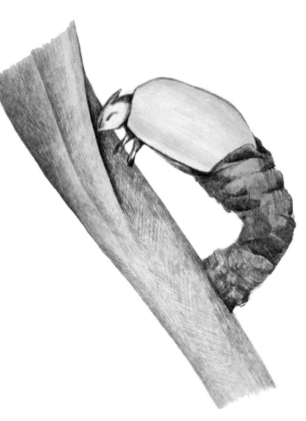

Out of the chrysalis

The ladybug is now ready to leave the chrysalis. It is like being born again. The ladybug will be an insect that flies, so its life in the world outside will be very different.

The astonishing change from larva to ladybug is called a metamorphosis. This means "change of shape."

Now we shall see how the ladybug comes out of the chrysalis to start its new life as a flying insect.

The ladybug wakes up and moves about inside the chrysalis. It thrusts itself forwards, then it pushes hard and splits open the chrysalis. It comes out through this opening, head first. Its body is covered with pale yellow wing cases. The ladybug is tired and has to rest for a while.

It now looks for a place where it can hang down and stretch its wings. It draws them out slowly from the wing cases. They are divided into parts with struts between them, like an umbrella. This means that they can be folded and unfolded without tearing. The ladybug spreads them out to dry and remains quite still for several hours. The wing cases harden. Their color changes to red with black spots.

The first flight

When its wings are dry the ladybug folds them back under the hard cases which protect them.

It has now passed through all the stages of growth. It is ready to explore a new world where it will be flying, as well as crawling along branches.

First it smells with its antennae. They are very important to the ladybug. They move slightly as they receive the scent from other ladybugs. They also pick up the scent from greenfly.

There are masses of greenfly to be found in the garden. The ladybug lifts its wing cases. Then it brings its wings out and unfolds them. Away it goes on its first flight. As it flies it makes a cheerful humming sound.

Many different ladybugs

Our picture shows a few of the many different kinds of
ladybugs that are found in countries all over the world.
You would never actually see them all together in one
place. The large green insect on the branch of the tree is
a praying mantis. Ladybugs should be careful not to get
in its way because it likes to eat them.

Birds are dangerous to ladybugs too. With their sharp
eyesight, birds can easily spot these brightly colored
little insects. When they have baby birds, they take
ladybugs back to the nest as food for the young.

The ladybug has no weapon it can use for attack. It is not like the bee or wasp with its sting, or the ant with its drop of poison.

It does have a way of defending itself though. It can make itself taste very unpleasant. Sometimes a bird that is about to swallow it will draw back in disgust and fly away to search for something tastier. Even the praying mantis will go back to hunting grasshoppers at times. The ladybug will then be safe for a while.

Life is certainly difficult for an insect as small as this. However, there is one good thing about being so small. It is easy to hide. A ladybug can slip into a tiny crack in the bark of a tree, or under the smallest leaf. These are both ideal hiding places.

The ladybug's friends

Ladybugs have many friends. All children love them.

Perhaps you have heard the popular old rhyme which children say when a ladybug settles on their finger. It goes like this: "Ladybug, ladybug, fly away home. Your house is on fire and your children may burn."

People are not afraid of them as they are of some other insects like spiders. Ladybugs are supposed to bring good luck and no one likes to kill them. They are known to be useful to man.

The ladybug is one of the insects that is not harmful to man. It actually helps him by eating the greenfly which damage his crops. There is an interesting story to be told about ladybugs. The date palms in the oases of Mauretania were being destroyed by greenfly. Somebody discovered that some ladybugs in Iran—black ones with three red spots—could feed on these greenfly. So experts set about breeding them and sent them to the oases by plane. With such a rich supply of greenfly to feed on, the ladybugs quickly settled down in their new surroundings and bred in great numbers. The date palms were saved.

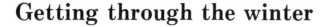

Getting through the winter

The first frosts of winter kill the greenfly. The ladybugs then have nothing to eat. However, they do not die. They hibernate, which means that they sleep for the winter. Long lines of them move along the tree branches and down the trunks looking for cracks in the bark. They crawl underneath and hide. There they remain until spring, keeping quite still and using no energy. They live off their stored fat.

Look at the picture on the next page. A ladybug has fallen on the path where the gardener is pushing his wheelbarrow. He did not see it and has pushed the wheel over it. Surely the ladybug has been hurt.

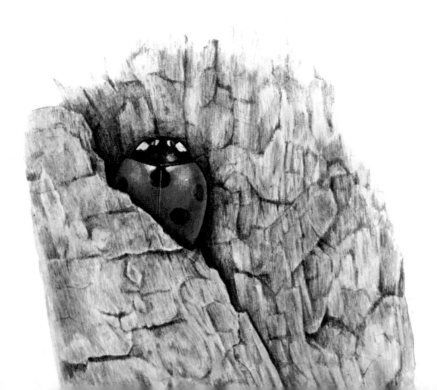

You would be wrong if you thought that the ladybug
was crushed by the wheel. Its shell is so hard that it can
bear an enormous weight. It is as hard as a tortoise's
shell. The ladybug is in a very open place though. There
it is prey to the birds. Luckily it is able to crawl into the
bushes where it will not be disturbed. It slips
underground. Between the roots, it immediately falls
asleep. Its body is quite still. It seems dead. Its legs
and its antennae are curled up. If you pick it up, it does
not move. Then, after a moment, it stirs feebly. The
warmth of your hand is beginning to wake it up.

Put it back in its hiding place. It is best to let it sleep.
If it did awaken, you would not be able to feed it and it
would die. Left alone, it can live without food, as nature
meant it to.

A different kind of shelter

The ladybug with two spots has found a different way of passing the winter. It must need more warmth, for it has hidden in the folds of a curtain. Do not disturb it—it is half asleep.

As soon as spring comes it will fly away into the open air and find a mate. Then it will lay eggs and more ladybugs will come from these just as it came from its own egg. This is what happens every spring.

SOME INTERESTING FACTS ABOUT LADYBUGS

Species:

The ladybug belongs to the beetle family. Ladybugs are known by the scientific name "Coccinellidae," which means "bright red." The word "beetle" comes from the Old English word "bitan" which means "to bite." This has to do with the way beetles take in food. We will discuss this later.

"Coleoptera" is the name given to the order of beetles. Beetles make up most of the insects of the world. There are approximately 290,000 types of beetles. This represents 40 percent of all insects.

Ladybugs live all over the world. There are 4,000 species of ladybugs. Most people are familiar with the red colored type. However, some are yellow, and some are black with red spots.

The feature which separates ladybugs from other types of insects is its "elytra." The elytra is the hard shell which covers the wings and part of the body.

Description:

The body of the ladybug is small and compact. Its head is very close to its body. The body is round in shape. It has no "waist" as many other insects. The body is clearly divided into the three main parts: the head, the thorax (or chest), and the abdomen. The ladybug has an "exoskeleton." This means that the hard part of the body is on the outside. By contrast, humans have their skeletons on the inside. The body is arched. Usually it is brightly colored.

The legs are short. There are three pairs, each ending in a jointed foot. Even though they have short legs, they are good runners. They are not very good flyers, though. Their wings do not beat fast enough. They beat 70 to 90 times a second. This is slow compared with a mosquito, which beats 280 to 310 times a second. They have compound eyes. That means that they have many lenses. When a ladybug looks at something it sees the same picture repeated again and again. The antennae hold the organs of touch and smell. Their antennae are divided into 10 or 11 segments. They are shorter than most other beetles.

Their blood is yellow-orange in color. Ladybugs have a defense mechanism called "reflex bleeding." When a ladybug senses that it is about to be attacked it squirts blood out from the knee. There is a substance in the blood which tastes very bad. Possible attackers seem to know this and leave the ladybug alone.

Even though it doesn't look it, the ladybug is a vicious hunter. It feeds on other insects. It eats aphids, mealybugs, scale insects, and snails. It will eat just about any insect it can kill. Its mouth is developed especially for this purpose. It has pincers. Pincers are like the claws of a crab. The ladybug uses these to grab its prey. It then makes a hole in the victim's body. With a special tube in its mouth it pours a liquid into the body. This liquid turns all the organs into a "soup." It then sucks the "soup" into its own body. The ladybug, as you see, eats its food already digested.

The "elytra" is the hard outer shell which protects the fragile wings and part of the abdomen. This elytra is amazingly strong. A ladybug can stand 800 times its own weight without cracking its shell! The elytra is one reason why the beetle is surviving so well all over the world. It gives the extra edge of protection which most insects do not have.

In winter, the insects which the ladybug feeds on disappear. In order to keep from starving the ladybug hibernates. Hibernation is the deep sleep which animals and insects go into during the cold months. The ladybug will find a crack in a tree and fall asleep. All its body systems will slow down. It almost looks dead. It does not eat. In spring it will awaken.

Family Life:

The ladybug develops from egg to adult by a process called "metamorphosis." This means "change of shape."

The shape of the ladybug certainly does change in this time.

Metamorphosis contains 4 stages: egg, larva, pupa and adult.

Egg stage:

The female lays already fertilized eggs. The male has already fertilized them and they are ready to develop. The eggs are long and bright yellow in color. There are hundreds of them in a batch. The female makes sure that she places her eggs on a plant where there are lots of aphids and greenflies for the babies to eat.

Larva stage:

The larva stage lasts for 4 or 5 weeks. At this stage they are called "grubs." They have carrot-shaped bodies with well developed legs. They need these to search for food. There are 6 legs, just like an adult. They eat the soft bodied insects that they find on the plant: greenflies, plant lice and scale insects. They will "molt," or shed their skins, three times. They do this as their bodies grow larger. At the end of the larva stage a sticky fluid will begin to cover their bodies. This is called a "chrysalis."

Pupa stage:

The pupa stage lasts for about 1 week. The chrysalis has now formed over the entire body. The pupa lives in the open air. It hangs head down from the leaf of a plant. In this stage the wings, legs and antennae are growing to full development.

Adult:

When the new adult emerges from the chrysalis it does not have its true color. The wings and elytra are a pale color. Only later will the familiar red background with black spots appear.

In warm climates ladybugs tend to reproduce more often. Generally there are two generations in one year.

Conservation:

The ladybug, like most beetles, is in no danger of extinction. In vast numbers, they are all over the world.

They are useful to farmers because they kill insects which are harmful to crops. In fact, in the western mountains of the United States, collections are made of hibernating ladybugs. They are sold to farmers to control crop eating pests. Some ladybugs were purposely introduced into this country. The Australian ladybug was brought to California to kill a plague of scale insects. Jacques ladybug started in Europe. It was also introduced in the United States. This is one time when more thought should have been given. Without natural enemies, it became a pest to the alfalfa crop.